YEAR 5

WRITING

NAPLAN*-FORMAT PRACTICE TESTS
with answers

Essential preparation for Year 5
NAPLAN* Tests in WRITING

Alfred Fletcher

CORONEOS PUBLICATIONS

* These tests have been produced by Coroneos Publications independently of Australian governments and are not officially endorsed publications of the NAPLAN program

YEAR 5 WRITING
NAPLAN*-FORMAT PRACTICE TESTS with answers
© Alfred Fletcher 2010
Published by Coroneos Publications 2010

ISBN 978-1-921565-46-5

* These tests have been produced by Coroneos Publications independently of Australian governments and are not officially endorsed publications of the NAPLAN program

THIS BOOK IS AVAILABLE FROM RECOGNISED BOOKSELLERS OR CONTACT:

Coroneos Publications
Telephone: (02) 9624 3 977   Facsimile: (02) 9624 3717
Business Address: 6/195 Prospect Highway Seven Hills 2147
Postal Address: PO Box 2 Seven Hills 2147
Website: www. coroneos.com.au or www.basicskillsseries.com
E-mail: coroneospublications@westnet.com.au

Contents

NOTE:

• Students have 40 minutes to complete a test.

• Students must use 2B or HB pencils only.

Introductory Notes and the NAPLAN* Test

This book is designed to help you practise for the Writing section of the NAPLAN* test and develop the skills necessary to competently handle any writing task presented to you at this stage of your development. To date the NAPLAN* test has been only a narrative but here we have included examples of other types of writing you will experience during your schooling. Practicing these will develop skills that will assist you in all areas of your writing.

Also included in this book are some hints on how to improve your writing. Follow these hints and use them in your work as they may assist you in gaining additional vital marks under examination conditions. They will also help you develop your vocabulary which is vital to good, concise and clear writing.

We wish you all the best for the exam and know that the activities and tasks in this book will assist you in reaching your writing potential.

The Writing Task

The NAPLAN* test includes a writing task which has been narrative based. A narrative is basically a story that is in time order and is used to entertain and emotionally change an audience. The narrative form follows a common pattern of orientation [introduction], complication [problem] and resolution [conclusion]. A narrative can also inform, persuade and just be for social purposes.

With a narrative you have a great choice of what to write and as long as you follow the basic pattern you can be as creative as you like. This gives you, as a writer, the opportunity to show the full range of your abilities creatively but also use a wide range of vocabulary, show solid sentence structure and paragraphing and develop character and setting for a particular audience.

The test will give you a topic such as space, animals, work or family. It will also give you some stimulus material on a sheet which may be images [pictures] and words or both. You can use these ideas in your story or can just use your own ideas. The choice is yours and you should decide this reasonably quickly so you can begin to write. You won't lose marks for using your own ideas.

Pay attention to all the instructions and use your planning time well. The instructions on the test may tell you to think about the characters you will use, the complication or problem and the end. It will also tell you to write in sentences, pay attention to vocabulary, spelling and punctuation. An instruction may also be that your work may be published so that you need to edit carefully.

Remember in the test you will have five (5) minutes of planning time. Then you will have thirty (30) minutes to write the narrative. Finally you will have five (5) minutes to edit your work. The editing process is important and you should use this time to check your work including spelling and punctuation. One easy structural thing to check is paragraphs. Look at your work to see if you have forgotten to use them in your rush to write your piece.

What Markers Look For When Examining Your Work

Of course your test will be marked and so it is good to know what the examiner or marker is looking for. Currently there are ten (10) criteria that are used for marking the writing task. These are shown below with the mark or score range shown for each one listed below.

☑	Audience	0-6
☑	Text structure	0-4
☑	Ideas	0-5
☑	Character and setting	0-4
☑	Vocabulary	0-5
☑	Cohesion	0-4
☑	Paragraphing	0-2
☑	Sentence structure	0-6
☑	Punctuation	0-5
☑	Spelling	0-6

Most of these terms are self explanatory but the term cohesion just means that your story holds together with one idea or line of thought. As you get older you will see the term 'sustained writing' which means much the same thing.

By understanding clearly the information you have just read you will have taken the first major step on your path to success in these tests. By knowing what you have to do you will be prepared for it and confident in what you need to do to succeed. Re-read these introductory notes several times. Then you know what to expect in the exam and won't be surprised by the words in the exam or the format. The next section gives you some writing tips to help improve your writing.

IMPROVING YOUR WRITING

Writing improvement is a matter of practice and developing your skills and vocabulary so you can express yourself clearly.

Writing the Correct Text Type

When you are asked to write in a particular text type make sure that you follow the correct structure or format for that type of writing. For example in a narrative you would use the structure: orientation, complication and resolution. Try to know all the different types and what is required. This book will help you to do that.

Ensuring Cohesion

To ensure that your story sticks together it is best to have one idea that holds the story together. If you have too many ideas your story will become confused and so will your readers or audience. Remember to stick to the topic or idea you are given in the stimulus material for the exam. Make sure the tense of the story is consistent and you have sustained the main idea.

Write in Paragraphs

One of the marking criteria for the exam is paragraphing and you should begin a new paragraph for a new thought or concept in your story. Shorter paragraphs are usually clearer and audiences like to be clear on what they are reading. If you get to the end of your story and begin to edit and notice you don't have paragraphs you can still put them in. To do this you can just put a [symbol before the word where a new paragraph starts. The marker will understand what you mean.

Engaging the Audience

To engage and entertain an audience a good introduction is necessary. It needs to be interesting and make the audience want to read on. You can practice this by writing different introductions to the same story and seeing which one your family and friends like best. The same idea is also relevant to the resolution. Audiences don't like stories which don't have an ending that solves the puzzle or complication in the story. Use the planning time to work out your ending.

Vocabulary

Vocabulary is a powerful tool for the writer to have. Word choices help expression and make your idea(s) easy for the audience to understand. To improve your vocabulary you can use a dictionary and a thesaurus to find new words. Make sure you understand what a word means before you use it and also how to use it correctly. Don't just use 'big' words to impress.

Sentence Structure

When you write your work make sure you write in sentences. As you learn to write you will use longer or compound sentences. Sentences should begin with a capital letter and end with a piece of punctuation such as a full stop or question mark. This will help the marker know you can use a sentence.

Spelling

Spelling is something that can be practised if you are not as strong in this area as you might be. Word lists can be useful and there are many good spelling books that can assist you in developing your skills. Don't be afraid to use new words as you can correct spelling in the editing process.

Characters

Characters are usually the people in your story. For a short story such as the one in the test you should not have too many characters. This is because you need to make sure your audience can follow a few characters without becoming lost. You can then also develop them better by using description and dialogue.

Setting

Setting is the place where your story happens. A story may have more than one setting. For example you could be out on a bushwalk in a forest and then travel home in a car. You should describe your setting so the audience know where they are and can imagine it more clearly. The markers will be looking that you have a setting so ensure your story has a place.

Editing

The editing process is an important one and you have five (5) minutes at the end of the test to edit. In your mind you should have a mental list of the areas the examiners are looking for and work on those. Think of things like tense and ask the question does my story have the correct structure. Re-read your work and fix little errors in the spelling, punctuation and grammar that may occur under exam conditions.

WRITING A NARRATIVE

The basic structure of a narrative is shown below:
orientation [introduction]
complication [problem]
resolution [conclusion]

Each of these MUST be included in your narrative or story. It is particularly important to have a strong introduction and resolution to leave your audience satisfied at the end of their reading. Remember that the purpose of a narrative is firstly to entertain but it can also inform, persuade and emotionally touch the audience.

In clarifying your thoughts on the structure an orientation tells the audience the WHO, WHERE and WHEN of the story while the complication is the problem that arises in the narrative. An orientation sentence might be: Sybil was walking along a winding, dirt track in the National Park west of Sydney.

The resolution or conclusion to your story needs to have a solution to the complication you have created. A complication to our story might be an unexpected storm that traps Sybil and the resolution might be her rescue by helicopter. The complication usually leads to the climax or most exciting part of the story.

The audience need to be engaged with the story and one way to do this is to have characters that the audience like. If they like your characters they will read on to find out what happens to them. To ensure your characters are engaging or interesting they need to share with the reader some feelings and thoughts. As a writer you can do this by using description and/or dialogue (conversation). If you can't think of a good description just use someone you know who might be like that character. With dialogue or conversation ensure that they speak correctly for their age.

It is important to focus on one main idea or theme in the story so as to remain consistent throughout the narrative. This will stop you and the audience becoming confused about a number of ideas. The planning time before you begin writing will help you decide on your idea and plan how you will maintain it. You only have thirty minutes to write so don't plan for too many characters and think about your resolution so you don't have to rush the ending and spoil the story.

The writing hints in the previous section apply here as well so you should check all those items in your editing. These include: spelling, punctuation. grammar, sentence structure, paragraphing, setting, character and cohesion.

OTHER TYPES OF WRITING

With all these types of writing the following hints apply. Check all these items in your editing. These include: spelling, punctuation. grammar, sentence structure, paragraphing, setting, character and cohesion. Of course some variations occur and these are explained below. These have already been discussed in detail and will not be repeated here.

Practice tasks are given for each of these types of writing later in the book. You will still need to write these under exam conditions and edit carefully. They are excellent practice to improve your skill areas.

Information Reports: these present facts and information. Here you can use sub-headings for different sections. You need to use clear, concise sentences under these sub-headings.

Recounts: a recount remembers or recalls events that have already happened. You will need to write these events in the time or chronological order in which they occurred but you can include some personal thoughts on the event. Usually an orientation tells the reader who, where and when.

Descriptions: a description gives details about the five senses (touch, taste, sight, sound and smell) but can also include emotions and/or feelings if necessary. You still need to orientate the reader in your description.

Discussions: a discussion will give different opinions about an issue or topic. They have an opening statement which gives the issue clearly and then some persuasive or emotive language is used to convince the audience about that view and its opposite view. Here the writer will also present evidence and finish with a recommendation.

You are about to write a story or narrative. The idea for your work is **'ADVENTURE'**.

Adventure can be very thrilling and rewarding but can also be dangerous and scary. Adventures can be anywhere even in a backyard and people can have them alone or with others. Some words to help you with your story are: **excitement, action** and **rushing**

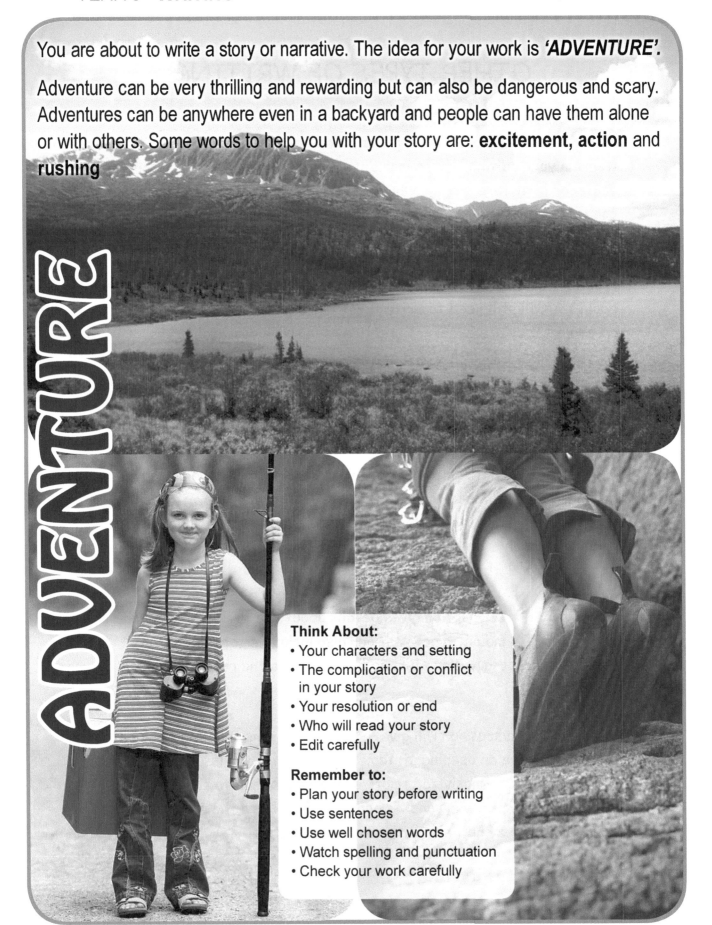

Think About:
- Your characters and setting
- The complication or conflict in your story
- Your resolution or end
- Who will read your story
- Edit carefully

Remember to:
- Plan your story before writing
- Use sentences
- Use well chosen words
- Watch spelling and punctuation
- Check your work carefully

Introduction
The orientation or introduction has the who, when and where of the story and a hint at the complication. Here it is a water filled ravine.

Here the plot begins to unfold.

Sets scene for the complication

It was a desperate situation with Melody caught in the ravine as it filled with water. The day had begun well with the whole White family walking in through the forest to the best trout stream in the Victorian Alps. The whole June long weekend had been set aside for the journey which held high hopes for the oldest White child to catch her first big brown trout.

Eagerly Melody had helped in preparation for the big event and she had also been practicing her casting. Melody had been fishing before but had not been to these mountains so it was a new experience. Her father had been before so he was the expert who guided them all in after they left the car.

The plan was to find one of the old huts that dotted these hills. They had been built by the stockmen who ran cattle and they were excellent rest spots near the river. They soon arrived and began to unpack their belongings. It was now late in the afternoon and there was no time for fishing by the time they set up camp and cooked dinner. That night around the fire they began to tell stories and sing songs. A happy time was had by all before a well deserved rest.

The next morning Melody and her dad, Jack, left the camp and her mum behind with her two little brothers. They had other plans for the day. The bush was thick but a windy track led them to the stream. Melody's dad told her to begin to cast her fishing line into the stream and follow it along the ravine searching for the big trout that she wanted.

Complication.

Here it is the change in the weather and Melody's father's injury.

He watched her carefully as she walked into the stream. The Australian bush was dangerous and he worried especially about poisonous snakes which infested the region. Another problem was becoming the quickly changing weather which had become windy and cloudy. It changed fast up in the mountains and people had been trapped before. Hurriedly he began to catch up to Melody, now not worried about scaring the fish.

Rain began to fall, lightly at first and then heavily with an increase in the wind. He told her they had to head back along the ravine but he slipped in and twisted his ankle. In pain he crawled to the shore and Melody followed him. He had a small medical kit and took out some aspirin and a bandage. This helped and they began to walk back.

Note how the tension builds to the resolution. The suspense keeps the reader interested

As the rain increased he noticed the water was rising and tried to hurry. It was hopeless and he asked Melody to help him to higher ground and they would use the emergency beacon in the pack. Unfortunately when he went to get it the beacon was gone. They decided it must've fallen out when he fell and Melody had to go back for it before the water rose too much.

She quickly headed for the now fast running stream and slushed through the water. Melody found the spot where he fell but the water had risen so she had to feel for it under the cold water. Scrabbling around she managed to grab it and head back. The water had risen considerably since she had left her father and it seemed she would be caught in the ravine, unable to get back. The shore was slippery so she kept along the edge of the water and headed back. She saw her father's bright orange jacket and was so relieved she had not been trapped.

Resolution
Here the story ends with a positive ending. The resolution can be negative or unhappy

She gave him the beacon and he set it off. They sat back in the rain and waited to be rescued. He told Melody she had been very brave and so did the men from the rescue party that came. They had to carry her father out in a stretcher as his ankle was broken not sprained. The walk out was in the rain but she felt safe with all the adults around her.

While Melody didn't catch her fish she certainly had an adventure and her mother said they would go back again one day and she would get her fish. Melody thought this was a good idea but said they needed to by a new emergency beacon before she would head out into the bush again!

Think About:
• Your characters and setting
• The complication or conflict in your story
• Your resolution or end
• Who will read your story
• Edit carefully

Remember to:
• Plan your story before writing
• Use sentences
• Use well chosen words
• Watch spelling and punctuation
• Check your work carefully

mystery

You are about to write a story or narrative.
The idea for your work is 'MYSTERY'.

The word mystery suggests a problem
to be solved. Perhaps there are clues
and people to help solve the mystery.
Mysteries are
not just about
crime and crimes
but can be about
any problem. Some
words to help you
with your story are:
discovery, shadows
and **investigate.**

MYSTERY

© Alfred Fletcher
Coroneos Publications

Think About:
• Your characters and setting
• The complication or conflict in your story
• Your resolution or end
• Who will read your story
• Edit carefully

Remember to:
• Plan your story before writing
• Use sentences
• Use well chosen words
• Watch spelling and punctuation
• Check your work carefully

STRANDED

You are about to write a story or narrative. The idea for your work is 'STRANDED'.

Being stranded usually means someone or something is alone somewhere in the world or perhaps on another world. Being stranded means that skills are put to the test. Their might be a rescue or not. Some words to help you with your story are: **lost, alone** and **survival.**

STRANDED

CREATE

Think About:
- Your characters and setting
- The complication or conflict in your story
- Your resolution or end
- Who will read your story
- Edit carefully

Remember to:
- Plan your story before writing
- Use sentences
- Use well chosen words
- Watch spelling and punctuation
- Check your work carefully

You are about to write a story or narrative. The idea for your work is 'CREATE'.

The word create brings to mind the making of things. When people create they make something original and often unique. The act of creating can be easy or difficult but often takes much time.. Some words to help you with your story are: **workshop**, **invention** and **money**.

CREATE

....

....

....

....

....

....

....

....

....

....

....

....

....

....

....

....

You are about to write a story or narrative. The idea for your work is **'HARBOUR'.**

A harbour is a geographical feature along a coast where boats are safe to anchor. Their can be quite large places built around them and many things can happen there. Harbours contain much sea-life and people use them a lot. Some words to help you with your story are: **ferry, headland** and **jetty.**

Think About:
- Your characters and setting
- The complication or conflict in your story
- Your resolution or end
- Who will read your story
- Edit carefully

Remember to:
- Plan your story before writing
- Use sentences
- Use well chosen words
- Watch spelling and punctuation
- Check your work carefully

HARBOUR

....

....

....

....

....

....

....

....

....

....

....

....

....

....

....

....

....

You are about to write a story or narrative. The idea for your work is **'ENVIRONMENT'.**

The environment is all around us and the word usually refers to the natural land and how it was before people came. Many people care about the environment and how we treat it. Another environment is the city and where we live. Some words to help you with your story are: **pollution, natural** and **caring.**

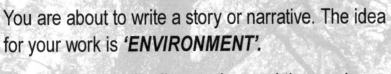

Think About:
- Your characters and setting
- The complication or conflict in your story
- Your resolution or end
- Who will read your story
- Edit carefully

Remember to:
- Plan your story before writing
- Use sentences
- Use well chosen words
- Watch spelling and punctuation
- Check your work carefully

© Alfred Fletcher
Coroneos Publications

ENVIRONMENT

© Alfred Fletcher
Coroneos Publications

You are about to write a story or narrative. The idea for your work is *'DISCOVERY'*.

A discovery is when you find something or learn something. A discovery can be very exciting and perhaps the discovery will get you something wonderful. Discoveries can also cause problems. Some words to help you with your story are: **treasure, journey** and **friendship.**

Think About:
• Your characters and setting
• The complication or conflict in your story
• Your resolution or end
• Who will read your story
• Edit carefully

Remember to:
• Plan your story before writing
• Use sentences
• Use well chosen words
• Watch spelling and punctuation
• Check your work carefully

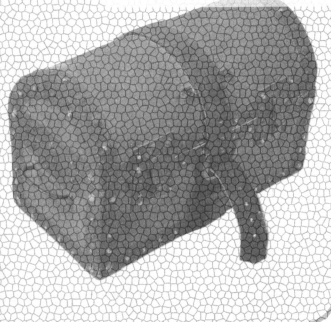

DISCOVERY

© Alfred Fletcher
Coroneos Publications

Writing Descriptions

A description gives details about the <u>five</u> <u>senses</u> (touch, taste, sight, sound and smell) but can also include <u>emotions</u> and/ or feelings if necessary. You still need to orientate the reader in your description.

The stimulus page opposite provides images of a holiday destination In the following pages there is an example of a description 'My Holiday Place'. There are two more descriptions for you to complete as well.

My Holiday Spot

You are about to write a description. The idea for your work is 'My Holiday Spot'.

A holiday spot can be any place that you go for a holiday. It could be a farm, the beach, a city overseas or to a relative's place.. Some words to help you with your story are: **activity, outdoors** and **aeroplane.**

Description 1: My Holiday Spot

Introduction:
Tells what is being described, why and when. Sets scene

After the plane landed we were taken to our holiday destination, the Bula Bula Resort in Fiji. From the hire car window I could see hundreds of coconut trees and vast sweeping lawns before the entrance which was shaped like a Fijian hut. Even the roof was thatched from leaves gathered from native vegetation.

Use of the senses Examples here are touch, sound, smell, feel and taste.

Inside it was luxurious and had many local artefacts on the walls. The lady at the front desk had a brightly coloured shirt on and she was very friendly as we collected the keys to our room. On the way we walked past the restaurant which had stunning food smells coming out of the kitchen. It made me feel hungry.

Body
Gives description of what the writer experiences

Our room was a large hut on the waterfront. It had three bedrooms and you could see the beach from the living room. It had umbrellas in the yellow-white sands and the water looked inviting after the long journey. My bedroom had a fan in the roof and a big double bed which was exciting.

Dad said we could all go down to the sandy beach so we clambered into our swimmers and headed off on the little track with was made of crushed shells. The water was cool and I could feel my skin lose the heat of the day. I asked if we could go snorkelling and Mum replied in the positive.

Word Choice
Use descriptive words like adjectives and adverbs. Give your own feelings

Underwater my eyes were dazzled by the array of coloured fish and corals. I felt some starfish and their skin was rough. We were even lucky enough to see some orange and blue seahorse attached to the seaweed just off the beach. We didn't touch these of course. After this we went back to the beach and I could taste the saltwater on my lips. With sand clinging to my wet feet we headed back to our hut.

Conclusion
Doesn't have to end like a story but you need to tell your audience the description is over.

The whole family sat on the porch and watched the sun set in the west and the colours reflected off the water. I had a fizzy coke with some melted ice-cream in it from the wet bar around the pool. It was very peaceful hearing the waves and I felt that this holiday was going to be the best ever.

My New Car

You are about to write a description. The idea for your work is 'The New Car'.

A new car often means a change for the better, and sometimes things become worse. There may be opportunities to do things that previously weren't possible. Some words to help you with your story are: **luxury, engines** and **lifestyle.**

The New Car

....

....

....

....

....

....

....

....

....

....

....

....

....

....

....

....

My Secret Place

You are about to write a description. The idea for your work is 'My Secret Place'.

Do you have a special place where you can go to do things all by yourself? Is it a shed in the back garden, or a treehouse or a room in your house where nobody else goes? Some words to help you with your story are: **solitude, thinking** and **observation.**

Description 3: My Secret Place

© Alfred Fletcher
Coroneos Publications

Year 5 WRITING
NAPLAN* Format Practice Tests

Writing Recounts

A recount remembers or recalls events that have already happened. You will need to write these events in the time or <u>chronological order</u> in which they occurred but you can include some <u>personal thoughts</u> on the event. Usually an orientation tells the reader who, where and when.

The stimulus page opposite provides images of sporting events. In the following pages there is an example of a recount 'My Day at the Beach'.

There are two more recounts for you to complete as well.

A Day at the Beach

You are about to write a recount. The idea for your work is 'A Day at the Beach'.

On a visit to the beach you might see people picnicing, seashells, sun umbrellas and ice-creams. It can rain at the beach or the clouds might come and spoil the day. Some words to help you with your recount are: **sunburn, waves** and **dolphins.**

Recount 1: My Day at the Beach

Introduction
Sets scene for what is happening in the recount and tells time and place etc

Time and place and what the recount is about.

Body
Tells what is happening in chronological order with some personal thoughts

Events of the day in order. Some description and action is used to interest the reader in the writing.

It was an uncomfortable and humid day as I headed down the street on our short walk to Nolan's Beach on the Mornington Peninsula. The sun was trying to get out from behind the heavy cloud cover. The beaches smell assaulted my nose as we got closer and it smelt good. I knew the sand would be warm even this early in the morning and the water cool.

The asphalt of the road was hot on my feet as I crossed it and jumped up the grey concrete gutter. I was on my own for the first time these holidays as the rest of the family had stayed at the hotel fearing it would storm. I thought I'd take the risk and they agreed I could go.

I laid my towel down and headed for the water. It was cool but not cold and I dived in and began to swim out past the small white water created by the waves breaking on the shallow shore. I caught wave after wave and had some of the best body surfing that I had experienced. The waves were long and solid pushing you along.

It was a great experience but as the beach filled with people the surf between the flags began to get crowded. I thought about moving to a better spot but remembered my parents warning about it being safer between the flags. I got out and went to my towel.

I dried off and lay on the beach for a while watching the families make sandcastles and eating their picnic lunches. It was nearly time for me to go but I decided to have another swim to cool down before heading back. The surf was stronger now and the lifesavers were shouting warnings to people who had ventured out too far. This was not going to be me on my first time alone at the beach so I was careful.

Conclusion
Finishes the recount and ends what happened

I headed back in to shore and dried off. I walked back to the hotel with the sand stuck between my toes. It had been a great morning but I was pleased to be going back to my family for lunch.

My Day at Work

You are about to write a recount. The idea for your work is 'My Day at Work'.

A day at work might be in the city at an office or in a factory. It could be on a farm or outdoors in the sun. Some people also work from home. Some words to help you with your recount are: **lunchtime, train** and **pens.**

Recount 2: My Day at Work

....

....

....

....

....

....

....

....

....

....

....

....

....

....

....

....

The Athletics Carnival

You are about to write a recount. The idea for your work is 'The Athletics Carnival'.

The athletics carvnival is usually held on an oval with a track. Other events like long jump have a sandy landing area. Everbody has fun and races around. Some words to help you with your recount are: **speed, effort** and **friends.**

Recount 3: The Athletics Carnival.

© Alfred Fletcher
Coroneos Publications

Year 5 WRITING
NAPLAN* Format Practice Tests

Writing Discussions

Discussions are used for deciding arguments A discussion has four parts:

1. An overview of the topic and some information

2. An overview of one point of view on the topic.

3. An overview of the other side of the topic

4. A summary of the information and a concluding comment

The first discussion is about fast food and a model answer is given to the question "Should Smoking be banned?"

Should Smoking be Banned?

You are about to write a discussion. The idea for your work is 'Should Smoking be Banned'.

Smoking is still common and we see ads to help adults stop all the time. Here you have a chance to write your thoughts. Some words to help you with your story are: **illness, smoke** and **doctor.**

Discussion 1: Should Smoking be Banned?

Introduction
Gives a general overview of the topic and some information.

The issue of smoking covers a wide number of different viewpoints but the two most vocal come from opposite ends of the argument with the anti-smoking lobby wanting smoking banned completely and the smokers wanting the freedom to smoke. The current laws do not ban smoking but limit it to outside buildings and not in any enclosed area. They are also banned in most parks near where children play.

Idea 1
Gives a general overview of one point of view on the topic.

The anti – smoking health groups cite much evidence in their case. For years smoking has been known to cause cancer, destroy lung tissue and cause severe health problems. All the statistics collected show the high incidence of early death for smokers and the high cost of keeping very sick smokers alive.

Smoking is also very anti-social with the smoke from cigarettes polluting and the ash and butts smelly and unsightly. Smoking also stains walls and curtains with a yellow stain, not to mention the teeth of the smoker. The experts all agree that smoking is so dangerous it should be banned.

Idea 2
Gives a general overview of the other side of the discussion

Smoking groups disagree and while they don't argue that smoking is good for you they claim they have the right to choose whether they smoke and it should not be banned. They claim that civil rights issues are involved and that they should be allowed to smoke in private designated areas.

Smokers also argue that to give up smoking is a very stressful and they should be allowed to smoke as it is their habit. Some proponents of this argument also claim smoking is good for weight loss and thin people are healthier. These smoker's rights groups especially support the concept of the cigar bar where people can go to smoke in private so they don't infringe the rights of non-smokers.

Conclusion
Gives a general summary of the information and makes a concluding comment.

The weight of the argument seems to be in favour of banning smoking because of the severe health issues that arise from smoking but authorities need to be careful about individual rights when making decisions.

Should Sport be Compulsory?

You are about to write a discussion. The idea for your work is 'Should Sport be Compulsory'.

Compulsory means evrybody has to do it. What do you think about that idea? Some students love sport and others don't like it. Some words to help you with your story are: **teacher, fitness** and **rules**.

Discussion 2: Should Sport be Compulsory?

....

....

....

....

....

....

....

....

....

....

....

....

....

....

....

....

....

Are Video Games Too Violent?

You are about to write a discussion. The idea for your work is 'Are Video Games Too Violent?'.

Most children have played video games in their lives. What type of games are there and do they have violence? Is this a good thing for children?. Some words to help you with your story are: **colourful, action** and **educational.**

Discussion 3: Are Video Games Too Violent?

Writing Information Reports

Information Reports present <u>facts and information</u>.

Here you can use sub-headings for different sections.

You need to use clear, concise sentences under these <u>sub-headings</u>.

The stimulus page opposite provides images of fish In the following pages there is an example of an **Information Report** about 'Australia'

There are two more **Information Reports** for you to complete as well.

Australia

You are about to write an information report. The idea for your work is 'Australia'.

Australia is a big country with many unique plants and animals. Australians are excellent at many things such as sports and agriculture Some words to help you with your information report are: **coast**, **city** and **people.**

Information Report 1: Australia

Introduction
Gives a general overview of the topic and some information.

Australia

Australia is both an island and a continent. It is the world's largest island and its smallest continent. As an island Australia is surrounded by water and one of the country's attractions is the Great Barrier Reef. The native or indigenous peoples are called Aborigines or Kooris. Settlers from other lands came to Australia just over two hundred years ago.

Sections with Sub-headings
Each section has a sub-heading which alerts the reader to the topic.

Unique Australian Animals

Because Australia has been an island for a long time some very unique animals have developed. One such animal is the kangaroo but the country also has the platypus and echidna. These animals are protected by law and are quite rare. A very popular animal is the koala which lives in eucalyptus trees and eats the leaves. Australia is a lucky country to have such rare animals

Life in Australia

About twenty million people live in Australia and most of them live on the coastline near the beaches. Her biggest city is Sydney but the capital of Australia is Canberra. Most people live in or near the cities for work but Australia has a big farming community and agriculture has always been a big industry as has mining. Australians love sport and have a national game, Australian Rules, which is played in every state.

Many people come to Australia to live because it is a capitalist democracy and very safe. This has meant the population is very mixed and people from every country in the world live here. It is a multi-cultural society and all religions are tolerated. These ideas are supported by laws.

Australia in the future

Australia continues to have lots of people coming here from overseas to live. The economy is solid and people have jobs. It has no history of violence and its peacefulness and geographic beauty will always make it a safe haven for people.

Language is very factual and not emotional or opinion

Conclusion May give some conclusions about the topic.

Horses

You are about to write an information report. The idea for your work is 'Horses'.

Horses are very popular animals and we see them in the city as well as on farms. they are useful animals for work and pleasure. Some words to help you with your information report are: **racing, saddle** and **patting.**

Horses

Frogs

You are about to write an information report. The idea for your work is 'Frogs'.

Frogs are amphibians and are born as tadpoles. we can find frogs in small ponds in cities or the great rivers around the country. frogs craok at night Some words to help you with your information report are: **moist, dam** and **cling.**

Information Report 3: Frogs

Narrative 1: Adventure

It was a desperate situation with Melody caught in the ravine as it filled with water. The day had begun well with the whole White family walking in through the forest to the best trout stream in the Victorian Alps. The whole June long weekend had been set aside for the journey which held high hopes for the oldest White child to catch her first big brown trout.

Eagerly Melody had helped in preparation for the big event and she had also been practicing her casting. Melody had been fishing before but had not been to these mountains so it was a new experience. Her father had been before so he was the expert who guided them all in after they left the car.

The plan was to find one of the old huts that dotted these hills. They had been built by the stockmen who ran cattle and they were excellent rest spots near the river. They soon arrived and began to unpack their belongings. It was now late in the afternoon and there was no time for fishing by the time they set up camp and cooked dinner. That night around the fire they began to tell stories and sing songs. A happy time was had by all before a well deserved rest.

The next morning Melody and her dad, Jack, left the camp and her mum behind with her two little brothers. They had other plans for the day. The bush was thick but a windy track led them to the stream. Melody's dad told her to begin to cast her fishing line into the stream and follow it along the ravine searching for the big trout that she wanted.

He watched her carefully as she walked into the stream. The Australian bush was dangerous and he worried especially about poisonous snakes which infested the region. Another problem was becoming the quickly changing weather which had become windy and cloudy. It changed fast up in the mountains and people had been trapped before. Hurriedly he began to catch up to Melody, now not worried about scaring the fish.

Rain began to fall, lightly at first and then heavily with an increase in the wind. He told her they had to head back along the ravine but he slipped in and twisted his ankle. In pain he crawled to the shore and Melody followed him. He had a small medical kit and took out some aspirin and a bandage. This helped and they began to walk back.

As the rain increased he noticed the water was rising and tried to hurry. It was hopeless and he asked Melody to help him to higher ground and they would use the emergency beacon in the pack. Unfortunately when he went to get it the beacon was gone. They decided it must've fallen out when he fell and Melody had to go back for it before the water rose too much.

She quickly headed for the now fast running stream and slushed through the water. Melody found the spot where he fell but the water had risen so she had to feel for it under the cold water. Scrabbling around she managed to grab it and head back. The water had risen considerably since she had left her father and it seemed she would be caught in the ravine, unable to get back. The shore was slippery so she kept along the edge of the water and headed back. She saw her father's bright orange jacket and was so relieved she had not been trapped.

She gave him the beacon and he set it off. They sat back in the rain and waited to be rescued. He told Melody she had been very brave and so did the men from the rescue party that came. They had to carry her father out in a stretcher as his ankle was broken not sprained. The walk out was in the rain but she felt safe with all the adults around her.

While Melody didn't catch her fish she certainly had an adventure and her mother said they would go back again one day and she would get her fish. Melody thought this was a good idea but said they needed to by a new emergency beacon before she would head out into the bush again!

Narrative 2: Mystery

Punter Posse was an old fashioned private detective who had so few jobs lately they had taken his furniture away to sell. Punter was well past his best because his age and methods were not in tune with the modern electronic times. He didn't understand anything about the internet or spying devices he just knew how to catch crooks the old fashioned way. Even his dress with the old style suit and hat matched with polished shoes didn't attract clients anymore. He had thoughts about retirement but dismissed them as he didn't have anywhere to retire too.

As he sat in his chair and thought of the old days he noticed some kind of smoke wafting past his window. Bored he looked out and saw it was coming from the room below which was rented by that strange couple. It didn't mean much that he thought they were strange as he didn't like many people anyway. Still he thought the room might be on fire and didn't want the building to burn down so he headed downstairs.

The smoke which had an odd smell was also coming out from under the door. As he knocked on the door he could hear noise inside the room. The situation began to interest him as the smoke was a bit of a mystery. The door opened and a short woman with a hanky over her mouth and nose answered. He asked if he could help and she said no. She told him it was a problem with the heater which had burnt some paper and things would be under control in a minute.

Old Punter wasn't as sharp as he used to be but he knew that in summer you didn't use a heater. He didn't trust her and so he barged in. The room was full of chemical stuff and he knew it was all bad. A man came at him and Punter only had to hit him once. The woman yelled something at him and ran off. Punter called the police and they sent the Dangerous Chemicals Squad.

The police chief said Punter was a hero as he had discovered a plot to develop chemical weapons. He was pleased because his detective business certainly picked up after that.

Narrative 3: Stranded

Nobody believed that Cordelia had been granted her greatest wish when her Beavis Bear was returned to her. Nobody could believe after twelve years and all that drama that they could be reunited. It truly was a miracle and an amazing story of survival for both of them.

It had all begun years before when Cordelia's parent's yacht had been wrecked off the Caribbean island of Barbados. They had escaped in the life-raft thinking she had been washed overboard, but she had been caught on the boat. Terrified and alone in the storm she had clung to Beavis as the yacht careered through the churning ocean waves. Frantic with fear she fell asleep clutching him and awoke to sunlight and land.

The yacht had been washed up on a small atoll and she had no idea what to do. Her only companion was Beavis and she talked to him like a friend. Cordelia lived on the yacht for a few days, eating the food that was in the pantry but it soon began to run out. She began to explore the island in the mornings and evenings when the sun wasn't too hot. She found some coconuts but couldn't crack them open so they sat where they fell. There was no water or food on the island so she used some fishing gear on the boat to try and get some fish. She copied what her father had done with the lines but had no luck.

After a week she began to fear she would die but tried to be brave. Beavis was always with her and it was his luck that had them rescued. She went outside on deck to get him in and she saw a ship heading at them. It was a search party looking for the yacht. She forgot about Beavis and ran to the beach. The boat landed and they took her to safety. She had been rescued and they told her she could use the radio to contact her parents.

In her excitement she forgot about Beavis but later asked her parents to go back to the island and rescue him. When they arrived he was gone just like the yacht. A typhoon had taken them both. That is why people said it was a miracle when the old sailor knocked on her door with Beavis. He had heard her story and found Beavis on a beach. Beavis was stranded no longer.

Narrative 4: Create

The old man's name was Joss Heep and he had spent years in isolation perfecting his secret process for creating gold from metal. He had made a fortune in inventions when he was young but had become obsessed with making gold from metal. This crazy idea had made him the laughing stock of the scientific world and he had gone off to live by himself in his country manor in Essex, England.

Years went by and he thought he was getting closer and closer to the solution to his problem. Joss spent all his waking hours working on the problem and he spent his fortune searching for the solution. His laboratory was lined with chemicals and tools that held many years of work. One summer's day he was working in the lab with the morning sun pouring through the window. It cast a golden glow on his work and he felt it was his lucky day.

Joss began to mix the chemicals he thought would be the solution. He measured accurately with his glass tubes and carefully put all the contents into one bowl. He heated his oven and went out to get some iron from the stable forge. During his absence the chemicals became heated by the fire and exploded in a flurry of liquid and smoke. When he had put out the fire he noticed the metal spoon he used for breakfast had gold spots on it. He was so excited he jumped around.

Carefully he began to mix again and this time deliberately heated up the metal to near boiling point and plunged the spoon in. It instantly turned to gold. He was a genius! He would be the world's richest man! Fabulous! Joss then went back to his study and wrote a letters to all the important people in London and Essex. He invited them to his manor for a demonstration. It would be a fantastic day.

On the day all the important people were there. Joss was about to begin the demonstration when a voice called stop. It was the police chief who had discovered a counterfeiting machine in the lab. Joss had been using it to finance his research. Unfortunately he was immediately arrested for forgery. No one would now believe he had discovered how to turn metal into gold and his hopes of wealth faded as he was taken to prison.

Narrative 5: Harbour

Cobra Harbour was always bursting with boats as it was the place all the mega-rich went to in the northern summer. It was nearly full as the Cranium IV edged into the harbour and took the prime mooring. The Cranium IV was owned by Chris Bollinger who was the world's richest man. He had come to town to race his yacht against the best in the world in the Cobra to Svengali Race which happened every year.

As the yacht rounded the point you could see her helicopter pad, games deck, speedboat, nightclub and outdoor movie deck. This yacht had it all and many people were jealous of his wealth and extravagance. Chris didn't care; he had made his money in publishing and was still gouging profits from his authors and the public. He knew he had enemies and just didn't care.

That night he went to the casino and lost thousands at poker before heading off to a nightclub. Arriving back at the boat near six in the morning he saw a sight that bothered him. The Cranium IV's launch dinghy was down in the water. Someone was going to pay for this. Angrily he stormed aboard and began to yell. No one was there and he began to search the yacht. Suddenly the engines started and the yacht began to head out to sea. Racing to the bridge he found it occupied by characters from all the novels and books he had published over the years. This was madness he thought and began to yell and scream at them.

The characters ignored him and kept heading out to sea. Eventually Chris calmed down and asked what they wanted. The main character, Dr Wavell Burgess, from his top detective series said they were going to leave him at sea in the dinghy to give him time to think about his greed and nasty manner with people. Chris laughed and said he was just fine. They turned and kept the yacht heading out. Chris began to rant and rave but they abandoned him fifty kilometres out to sea.

He was out there for days but eventually was rescued by a passing ocean liner. No one believed his story and the doctors thought he'd had a breakdown. Whatever had happened they liked the new Chris Bollinger who indeed had changed his ways and was now kind and generous to all.

Narrative 6: Environment

Doom and gloom was all Alexis ever heard from her sister, Stephanie, since she had joined the Green Movement group. They were a bunch of crazy environmentalists who were overly concerned about the planet. Alexis was tired of being lectured about global warming, the coral reefs, footprints and how we were all going to die. It was boring. She told Stephanie in anger one fine winter's morning to stop being so negative and do something if she was so concerned about the planet.

Stephanie was quite upset and picked up her Greens Party pamphlets and stormed into her room. She thought about her sister's comments for a while and realised that greenies did whine a lot and she was becoming just like them. So she decided to act. She called out to Alexis that she was going to clean up the local creek near their house and if Alexis wanted to help she was welcome. As a conciliatory gesture Alexis said she would come, secretly pleased Stephanie had decided to be positive for a change. They grabbed some garbage bags and headed off to the creek. On the way Stephanie said she was going to stop moaning and start doing unlike most of her unemployed Green Movement friends.

At the creek they spent hours picking up rubbish in bags. Even Alexis was surprised at the amount of rubbish. Near the end of the creek deep in the bush they heard a splashing noise. Coming around the bend they saw an old ute and some bloke with a gas mask on dumping drums of waste into the creek. They yelled out and the startled man took off leaving his drums of waste pouring into the creek.

The girls ran over but the smell was horrible. They raced back to the houses and ran home. Here they called the police and said they would head back to show them the spot. The girls led the police and a crew from the Environmental Protection Agency to the spot. They sealed off the area and tried to contain the toxic spill. The police began to investigate immediately and three days later a man was arrested as they had traced the chemicals to a local factory. Stephanie was so pleased she had acted and Alexis decided that saving the environment wasn't such a bad thing after all.

Narrative 7: Discovery

What a moment. What a day. What shock was going to happen next? Pasha had never before had so many important choices thrown at her. In the space of a day she had discovered she had a sister, came from a wealthy family and now had to choose what she was going to do with the rest of her life. What more could happen?

As she walked away from the house with her new sister, Sophia, Pasha was in a state of shock. She thought back to the discovery of the old chest in the attic of her adoptive parent's home. Why had no one told her it was her legacy? Why had they kept its contents a secret for all these years? Too many questions for one day and she now had to get some answers as she looked across at Sophia, her dark haired twin.

Pasha asked Sophia what she knew about it all and she began to tell the whole tale. They had been separated at birth as their mother was too young and poor to keep them. Both girls had been given out for adoption but after Pasha was taken away their mother was so heartbroken she ran out of the hospital with Sophia and kept moving for the next 15 years. During this time, Sarah, their mother, had created an on-line business selling make-up. It helped them survive over the years. She had sold it in the dot-com boom and they were now very wealthy.

Unfortunately Sarah had recently been killed in a car accident and Sophia had inherited the leather chest. Inside was the story of her family situation and the fact she had a twin sister. Sophia immediately began to search for her sister who had the same type of leather chest but with different contents that her mother had prepared to be sent with her on adoption. It took two years for Sophia to find her sister but now they were together and they both wanted to look in the chest.

Giving each other a hug for strength they headed back to the house to unravel the next mystery. Who knew what they would discover in the chest, perhaps more secrets, but at least they were together and together they would be strong.

Desciption 1: My Holiday Spot

After the plane landed we were taken to our holiday destination, the Bula Bula Resort in Fiji. From the hire car window I could see hundreds of coconut trees and vast sweeping lawns before the entrance which was shaped like a Fijian hut. Even the roof was thatched from leaves gathered from native vegetation.

Inside it was luxurious and had many local artefacts on the walls. The lady at the front desk had a brightly coloured shirt on and she was very friendly as we collected the keys to our room. On the way we walked past the restaurant which had stunning food smells coming out of the kitchen. It made me feel hungry.

Our room was a large hut on the waterfront. It had three bedrooms and you could see the beach from the living room. It had umbrellas in the yellow-white sands and the water looked inviting after the long journey. My bedroom had a fan in the roof and a big double bed which was exciting.

Dad said we could all go down to the sandy beach so we clambered into our swimmers and headed off on the little track with was made of crushed shells. The water was cool and I could feel my skin lose the heat of the day. I asked if we could go snorkelling and Mum replied in the positive.

Underwater my eyes were dazzled by the array of coloured fish and corals. I felt some starfish and their skin was rough. We were even lucky enough to see some orange and blue seahorse attached to the seaweed just off the beach. We didn't touch these of course. After this we went back to the beach and I could taste the saltwater on my lips. With sand clinging to my wet feet we headed back to our hut.

The whole family sat on the porch and watched the sun set in the west and the colours reflected off the water. I had a fizzy coke with some melted ice-cream in it from the wet bar around the pool. It was very peaceful hearing the waves and I felt that this holiday was going to be the best ever.

Description Two – The New Car

When Dad brought home our new car from the dealership I was so excited as it meant big trips into the bush. It was a brand new Mordent Bushwrecker Four Wheel Drive with all the extras. When I saw the big bullbar come around the corner of the street I rushed out to examine it carefully. The engine ticked noisily as it cooled down and I stood next to the large rubber all terrain wheels that would take us exploring.

The paint work was metallic blue and the interior colour was a fawny brown. The leather seats smelt that brand new smell that cars have when they haven't been used. Dad and I began to take the plastic wrapping off them so we could have a good look. I was allowed to sit in the front seat while he showed me the dashboard equipment. The seat was so soft and comfortable to sit on. I felt like I was floating.

When he turned the lights on the front of the car lit up like the main street of town. The car had buttons for everything and a really cool sound system with an Ipod dock for music. Dad made me look at the special present he had included in the extras package for me. In the back was a DVD screen so I could watch as we went along. The screen was sixteen centimetres across so it would be great viewing. This car had everything!

Mum came out with a cool drink and I could feel the ice on my tongue. Dad told her she could cool the drinks in the car esky which ran off the battery. She got in and I crawled over into the back. As I looked over the back seat I could see the carpeted boot which was huge. It had a black carpet which didn't feel all that soft, not like the seats. From my seat I looked at the silvery controls and touched each one to see what it did. I could set my own DVD's and control the windows. I even had my own hidden compartment and power supply.

I knew this was going to be my favourite car from then on. I was so happy holidays started next week so we could test it out.

Description 3: My Secret Place

Nestled, nearly hidden, high up in the Plane Tree in my yard is my tree house. It is tucked into a huge fork in the main trunk of the tree. Dad and my brother, Joshua, helped me build it, but it's mine and I spend a lot of time up the tree watching the world and reading. The tree house is about 10 metres high and we made a ladder to get to it using rope and leftover wood from the construction of the tree house.

The tree is huge and Dad said not to climb to the top. It is a deciduous tree which means it drops all its very green, flat leaves in the autumn. This is when you can see my tree house as it is not hidden. The branches are thicker than my arm and it is very safe to climb, especially the thick trunk which I can't put my arms around. When you climb it the tree feels so rough and smells like fresh crushed leaves.

The house itself is made from scrap wood from Dad's building sites and some old roofing off a house he demolished. The roofing is a little bit rusty and reddish not silver as it should be but it keeps the rain out. We also made a door frame which has half a door in it so I can look out over the top. Two windows are in either side to let light in and we put clear Perspex in them for safety. It feels and looks like glass so that's good. We have a wooden floor and it is very safe, especially as the rain can't get to it.

From the doorway I can see our brick house and all the way to the river. In the other direction I can see all the way to the city on a clear day but often it is invisible because of the grey-brown smog that covers it. I am allowed have two friends up here and we often have a tasty snack as we play and talk. All my friends think it is the best to have such a cool hideout.

I enjoy my tree house and wouldn't swap it for anything.

Recount 1: My Day at the Beach

It was an uncomfortable and humid day as I headed down the street on our short walk to Nolan's Beach on the Mornington Peninsula. The sun was trying to get out from behind the heavy cloud cover. The beaches smell assaulted my nose as we got closer and it smelt good. I knew the sand would be warm even this early in the morning and the water cool.

The asphalt of the road was hot on my feet as I crossed it and jumped up the grey concrete gutter. I was on my own for the first time these holidays as the rest of the family had stayed at the hotel fearing it would storm. I thought I'd take the risk and they agreed I could go.

I laid my towel down and headed for the water. It was cool but not cold and I dived in and began to swim out past the small white water created by the waves breaking on the shallow shore. I caught wave after wave and had some of the best body surfing that I had experienced. The waves were long and solid pushing you along.

It was a great experience but as the beach filled with people the surf between the flags began to get crowded. I thought about moving to a better spot but remembered my parents warning about it being safer between the flags. I got out and went to my towel.

I dried off and lay on the beach for a while watching the families make sandcastles and eating their picnic lunches. It was nearly time for me to go but I decided to have another swim to cool down before heading back. The surf was stronger now and the lifesavers were shouting warnings to people who had ventured out too far. This was not going to be me on my first time alone at the beach so I was careful.

I headed back in to shore and dried off. I walked back to the hotel with the sand stuck between my toes. It had been a great morning but I was pleased to be going back to my family for lunch.

Recount 2: My Day at Work

One week Mum had to go to a business conference and Dad and I were left alone for a week in the holidays. One Tuesday my sitter didn't arrive and rang in sick. That meant Dad had to take me to work with him. He made me put on my fluoro work shirt and take my hard hat as he was project managing a huge high rise development in the city near Rose Bay. We left immediately in his new ute and headed into the city.

Parking near the site office he took me by the hand and took me inside to introduce me around. The site secretary, Julie, gave me a coke from the fridge and I got to sit outside on some framing that was waiting to be sent up on the crane. My hard hat was a bit big for me but one man came past and tightened the band. He also gave me a BLF sticker to put on the front. Dad laughed when he saw it and said I had joined the union so now I didn't have to work.

I walked around with Dad all day and he was always talking to the other men often about safety up high. Once he went up and left me in the office which wasn't much fun. At lunchtime he sent the apprentice over to the shops and he came back with some hamburgers and chocolate milk for us. That was excellent and it was the best lunch. We ate good food when Mum was away but Dad told me not to tell her about it.

After lunch we walked around the site and then a man came over and said the safety scaffolding was now erected around the whole top floor. Dad told me for a treat I could go up with him to inspect it. We got into the elevator and put a safety harness on before heading up. At the top we walked near the edge but not too close as Dad said we had to be careful. I thought I could see to the edge of the country from up there. It was a magic moment to be up so high.

That was the end of my day and we soon headed down and got in the car for the journey home. I didn't think the day could be any better until Dad pulled into McDonalds for dinner!

Recount 3: The Athletics Carnival

I had to put my tracksuit on before I left home for school as the autumn weather was coolish and it had been raining. Brisbane Waters Primary always had its athletics carnival on the second Thursday of May every year and this was the fifth one I had been to. I loved the carnival as it was a day off school and I got to run around. I wanted to win at least one race so I could go to the district carnival and have another day off.

At the school oval we had to sit in our house groups and it was lucky my best friend Simone was in my house, Waratah. I wore the red colours in each race and when the eleven years girls' hundred metres was called I tore my tracksuit off and headed for the marshalling area. This year there were no heats just a final as many girls didn't want to run. We lined up at the start and I jumped quickly when I heard the starting gun go off.

My feet pounded the grass as I gave it my best. As I crossed the finishing line I was so puffed that I didn't know if I had won or not. Ms Finglestein came over and gave me the blue stick which signified first. My friends clapped me and Mrs Khan came over and congratulated me as she was house leader. I was puffed but excited. Now I had to prepare for the field events like high jump and discus. I placed second in both these events and now it was time for lunch.

I didn't eat much even though I was hungry as I had the eight hundred metres after lunch break and I didn't want to feel sick. We all sat and talked through lunch and then the races were called. After a bit of a wait my race began and you had to go three times around the big oval. It was so tiring but I managed to get past my main rival Ginnie Stowe near the finish to come first. Everyone was cheering and I was thrilled to have won the race for the first time.

Tired but satisfied with my efforts I helped the teachers pack up all the athletics equipment into the shed. We then lined up for the buses and headed home. I really wanted to tell my parents and big sister how well I had done at the carnival.

Discussion 1: Should Smoking be Banned?

The issue of smoking covers a wide number of different viewpoints but the two most vocal come from opposite ends of the argument with the anti-smoking lobby wanting smoking banned completely and the smokers wanting the freedom to smoke. The current laws do not ban smoking but limit it to outside buildings and not in any enclosed area. They are also banned in most parks near where children play.

The anti – smoking health groups cite much evidence in their case. For years smoking has been known to cause cancer, destroy lung tissue and cause severe health problems. All the statistics collected show the high incidence of early death for smokers and the high cost of keeping very sick smokers alive.

Smoking is also very anti-social with the smoke from cigarettes polluting and the ash and butts smelly and unsightly. Smoking also stains walls and curtains with a yellow stain, not to mention the teeth of the smoker. The experts all agree that smoking is so dangerous it should be banned.

Smoking groups disagree and while they don't argue that smoking is good for you they claim they have the right to choose whether they smoke and it should not be banned. They claim that civil rights issues are involved and that they should be allowed to smoke in private designated areas.

Smokers also argue that to give up smoking is a very stressful and they should be allowed to smoke as it is their habit. Some proponents of this argument also claim smoking is good for weight loss and thin people are healthier. These smoker's rights groups especially support the concept of the cigar bar where people can go to smoke in private so they don't infringe the rights of non-smokers.

The weight of the argument seems to be in favour of banning smoking because of the severe health issues that arise from smoking but authorities need to be careful about individual rights when making decisions.

Discussion 2: Should Sport be Compulsory?

Sport is a compulsory subject in Australian schools for many good reasons such as health and lifestyle issues but some groups have challenged this fundamental cornerstone in education as discriminatory and unnecessary in the modern world. Educational authorities are now fielding more complaints in schools and at higher levels from groups opposed to sports including physical education.

Sport has been compulsory in schools for many years. This includes physical education and dance which are used to teach children the benefits of a healthy lifestyle and expose them to different skills. Sport encourages activity and teaches co-ordination and other fundamental life skills in a positive environment. Their can be no doubt that these programs in all levels of schooling have contributed to a better lifestyle education and more awareness on health issues as well as giving children both practical and theoretical skills. These activities have been a core element in education for a century and their role has never been questioned until recently.

In the past few years some minority parental and religious groups have begun a campaign to remove sport from the curriculum and completely stop the teaching of personal health and sexuality issues. They claim that these should be taught in the home and that parents are the best placed to do this. Many also claim that sport is demoralising for those students who have few skills in this area and they should not be forced to participate. Some families have withdrawn students from sporting carnivals in protest and have made a case for alternative work during physical education. To date educational authorities have not bowed to these minority elements but some concessions have been made.

Overall sport and physical education are positive experiences for the majority of children and they need to be continued as part of a balanced program of education while some allowances can be made for special cases.

Discussion 3 : Are Video Games Too Violent?

The use of video games and gaming consoles in general has increased significantly over the past decade and while there are game content controls some groups claim it is not enough and their needs to be stricter control over game content. They cite the violence and sex that is openly available in easily purchased games and the obsessive natures of the gamers who live to play as examples of the need for more controls. Gamers on the other hand say that it is just a fantasy world and that it bears no relationship to the real world. The violence is all unrealistic and they can control what they do.

Family groups and media content analysts suggest that the violence in these games is too realistic and encourages children not only to be violent but to see violence as an abstract principle which numbs them to it. They use as examples hundreds of games where you can blow up, smash, shoot, stab and maim any number of people without consequence. In some games you can even destroy cities and whole planets in the most deadly manner. Surely children should not be subject to such violence constantly and their time would be better spent in outdoor and/or educational pursuits, especially as this violence has been linked to mass killings in the real world.

Gamers and rights activists claim that these games are not real and are purely for entertainment. They also state that the current controls are more than adequate and the PG and M and MA levels all indicate to parents whether the game is suitable for their child. They also point to the skills that these games develop especially the hand-eye co-ordination and the problem solving nature of many tasks. Supporters of this view also direct people to the educational use of many games and their use in schools. Many games are also hugely popular and bring people together on the internet in game rooms and forums.

Overall it needs to be said that games are very popular with today's youth but their does need to be some controls over access to the more violent, horrific and sexual games for younger gamers.

Information Report 1: Australia

Australia is both an island and a continent. It is the world's largest island and its smallest continent. As an island Australia is surrounded by water and one of the country's attractions is the Great Barrier Reef. The native or indigenous peoples are called Aborigines or Kooris. Settlers from other lands came to Australia just over two hundred years ago.

Unique Australian Animals

Because Australia has been an island for a long time some very unique animals have developed. One such animal is the kangaroo but the country also has the platypus and echidna. These animals are protected by law and are quite rare. A very popular animal is the koala which lives in eucalyptus trees and eats the leaves. Australia is a lucky country to have such rare animals

Life in Australia

About twenty million people live in Australia and most of them live on the coastline near the beaches. Her biggest city is Sydney but the capital of Australia is Canberra. Most people live in or near the cities for work but Australia has a big farming community and agriculture has always been a big industry as has mining. Australians love sport and have a national game, Australian Rules, which is played in every state.

Many people come to Australia to live because it is a capitalist democracy and very safe. This has meant the population is very mixed and people from every country in the world live here. It is a multi-cultural society and all religions are tolerated. These ideas are supported by laws.

Australia in the future

Australia continues to have lots of people coming here from overseas to live. The economy is solid and people have jobs. It has no history of violence and its peacefulness and geographic beauty will always make it a safe haven for people.

Information Report 2: Horses

Types of Horses

There are many types of horses but the best known is the thoroughbred which is used for horse racing. These horses can be quite highly-strung and sensitive so you need to be a good rider to have one. Other riding type horses are the Arab and Anglo Arab, the Warmblood, the Welsh Mountain Pony and the Quarter Horse. Shetland Ponies are a smaller horse and Clydesdale's are huge horses meant for work like pulling ploughs.

Choosing a Horse

Of course you need to decide what you want your horse for before you decide to buy one. Is it for riding or work? Other considerations are size, age, sex and the general condition of the horse. Think also of your own abilities and needs. When buying a horse you need to be careful to check its conformation and soundness.

Feeding a Horse

Feeding a horse can be as easy as leaving it in a grassy paddock and supplementing this with some hay but for horses that are in training you need to do more. They will require a special feed mix with lucerne chaff and hay, wheaten chaff and perhaps bran. They will also need a vitamin supplement, salt and maybe some pollard or grains.

Equipment for your Horse

The basic equipment for your horse is a saddle, mounts and stirrup leathers, saddlecloth, bridle and bit, helmet and riding boots, lead and headstall and brushes.

Overview

If you have all these things you will be able to enjoy your healthy, happy horse for many years.

Information Report 3: Frogs

Frog or Toad?

There are many frogs in Australia with possibly the most common being the Green Tree Frog which is very popular as a pet. We also have one toad which is the imported Cane Toad (Bufo Marinus) which has become a great pest across Australia.

What Frogs Eat

Frogs are carnivores and they will eat almost anything that moves if they can fit it in their mouth. Frogs like moving food and catch their food with the tongue, which is sticky. They catch the food and will use the front hands to stuff it in. they eat all kinds of insects, spiders, small reptiles and other frogs. Frogs will also eat moths and that is why you see them on windows around lights at night.

Life Cycle of a Frog

Frogs lay eggs in water usually around reeds or logs. Often they look like foam or gel. They will hatch as long as the eggs are moist. The eggs hatch as tadpoles which are not like frogs at all but more like fish. They can't leave the water and eat decaying plants in the water. As the tadpole gets older they grow arms and legs and lose their tail. They then are frogs and eat what a frog eats.

How do I Keep Frogs?

You need a license to keep frogs in many states but the essential equipment for frogs is a terrarium or fish tank which a filter for the water and a heater in cold areas. Frogs need humidity and space as well as regular food. They need some plants or wet rocks to hide in as well.

Conclusion

Frogs are wonderful animals but many are endangered because of the changing environment.